BREAKING THE SILENCE

Human rights violations based on sexual orientation

An AIUSA Report
ISBN: 0-939994-86-0
First published in February 1994
Amnesty International Publications
322 Eighth Avenue
New York, NY 10001

Table of contents

1
Protecting the Human Rights of All People

—In Brazil, the headless body of a local politician is found, mutilated and decapitated, in a garbage heap following his public announcement of his bisexuality and a political battle to remove him from office;
—In Greece, the editor of a gay and lesbian magazine is sentenced to five months in prison and a fine for publishing a comment questioning why so many men wanted to correspond with lesbians—the court ruled that the comment offended public feelings of decency and sexual morals;
—Two gay male activists and AIDS educators are harassed, arrested, and beaten based on trumped-up charges by authorities in Mexico;
—In the USA, a woman loses custody of her own child because a Virginia judge decides that as a lesbian she is by definition an unfit mother—using the fact that it is a crime in that state to have same-sex relations;
—In Colombia, "death squads" routinely target and kill gay men and transvestites as local authorities promote what they grotesquely term "*limpieza social*"—"social cleansing". The "death squads" operate without fear of prosecution: the gunmen themselves are often police officers;
—In Iran, the authorities reiterate publicly that death is a possible punishment for persons found guilty of homosexual acts.

Despite giant steps taken internationally and locally to make governments and individuals aware of the need to protect human rights, many people still live in fear that they will be arrested, tortured, or put to death by their own government. These are some of the abuses that Amnesty International was formed to combat.

Many people live in hunger, vulnerable to exploitation, in flight from their own countries or homes fearing public or domestic violence, rape, or murder without hope of protection or relief from the authorities, despite governmental obligations to ensure these rights. Too many men and women live in fear for their homes, their families, even their lives simply because of who they are—a H'mong hill woman, a Baha'i man, a woman with AIDS, a man in a wheelchair, a Latina lesbian, an Amadi boy, a female trade unionist, a Hutu farmer, a gay teacher.

The United Nations, through its founding pledge in its Charter, as well as in the Universal Declaration of Human Rights and a host of more specific human rights treaties, promises to respect and ensure the human rights of **all persons**. However, for a significant part of the world's population, this pledge has never been realized—or even acknowledged.

Governments at the recent 1993 World Conference on Human Rights re-affirmed the indivisibility and universality of all human rights—civil, political, economic, social, and cultural—and in affirming the Conference slogan of "all human rights for all people" took steps to remedy the historic neglect of the human rights of some groups, such as women. However, the final document of the Conference—the Vienna Declaration and Programme of Action—made no reference to the historic neglect of the human rights of lesbians, gay men, and bisexuals.[1]

Homosexuals in many parts of the world live in constant fear of government persecution—afraid that their private acts of love and public acts of courage will be punished by governments in secret torture chambers, at clandestine "safe houses," and on midnight raids. Many live in constant fear that lives lived behind or beyond closet doors will be snuffed out by government oppression.

The human rights movement has always been led by the actions of courageous individuals and groups, and the struggle for human rights for lesbians and gay men is no different. Local groups, national coalitions, and organizations have joined in the struggle to make real the pledge of "all human rights for all people" because "when governments ignore their responsibility to one sector of society, no one's human rights are safe."[2]

Lesbians and gay men have been part of the fight to protect human rights in local and national movements all over the world. Just as the struggle for human rights for women, for people living under apartheid, for indigenous peoples, for refugees, for the disappeared, and for the survivors of torture can not and should not be waged only by those people themselves, but by all of us, so too, the struggle to protect the basic human rights of lesbians and gay men must be waged by all of us.

In the major paper drafted by AI for the World Conference of Human Rights on the proposals for improving the protections of human rights in the United Nations, AI explicitly noted "vulnerable groups which require greater attention within the human rights program include children, indigenous peoples, the disabled, religious, ethnic, sexual and linguistic minorities and those afflicted by HIV and AIDS." This campaign seeks to begin to fulfill that call to action. By participating in this work to protect the human rights of gay men and lesbians, we hope to help in the realization of the goal of "all human rights for all."[3]

There are often inter-locking prejudices and discriminations which underlie execution, torture, and detention. The International Convention on the Elimination of All Forms of Racial Discrimination and the Covention on the Elimination of all Forms of Discrimination against Women provide an important international framework for combatting these violations. For example, a woman in prison may be raped not only because she is female, but because she is known to be a lesbian, and the action is specifically targeted at breaking down her sexual identity. Though both men and women may be raped in detention, a form of torture, men do not face the additional implications of pregnancy. The abuses faced by a lesbian, and her legal status to challenge them, may be different simply because of her gender. Likewise, a gay man may be the target of physical abuse by police officers because he is known to be a homosexual and is assumed to be a carrier of the AIDS virus. The incorrect linkage of HIV status and identity leading to abuses is not limited to gay men. Entire nationalities and ethnic groups have also been wrongly stigmatized in the global AIDS pandemic, as continuing ignorance and fear about the disease perpetuates misconceptions and violations.

A role for Amnesty International (AI) in protecting the rights of gays and lesbians

As a grass-roots, international human rights organization, AI has a particular and useful role to play in locating gay and lesbian rights in the consideration of human rights generally—not as special rights, but as fundamental rights ensured to each and every member of society.

A part of AI's overall goal is to defend the right of all persons to physical and psychological integrity and to work against grave violations of these rights. As sexual orientation is a fundamental dimension of human identity, the work of AI can contribute to the full protection of people, in their most basic and private selves, as well as in their public identities. Educating the public about the core nature of human rights work—protecting and promoting the inherent dignity of the person free from fear of governmental persecution—is an essential part of AI's mission.

While the mandate of Amnesty International focuses on a few select rights, the organization supports and seeks to strengthen the international structures protecting the full range of human rights, economic, social, and cultural as well as civil and political. Human rights awareness and education on all these issues can comprise an important part of the work of AI human rights activists in their own countries.

In order to work effectively to protect the human rights of all persons, Amnesty International has evolved over more than thirty years, both in the focus of its mandate and in the forms of its actions. AI has always opposed the torture and execution of anyone for any reason. In 1979 AI affirmed that those imprisoned for advocating gay rights would be taken up as prisoners of conscience and in 1982 the organization condemned the forcible "medical" treatment carried out on people in detention against their will for the purpose of altering their sexual orientation. In 1991 the organization expanded its mandate with regard to work on behalf of imprisoned homosexuals. AI will now consider for adoption anyone who is imprisoned solely because of their homosexuality, including the practice of homosexual acts in private between consenting adults. Since that time AI has documented gross violations of human rights against lesbians and gay men throughout the world. This report is a survey of these abuses and is not meant to be an exhaustive analysis of human rights violations against gays and lesbians worldwide.

Amnesty International's mandate and abuses against lesbians and gay men

Within its mandate, AI works for the release of prisoners of conscience—men and women detained solely for their beliefs, color, sex, ethnic origin, language or religion and who have not used or advocated violence. Included in this definition of "prisoner of conscience" are men and women detained solely by reason of their actual or alleged homosexuality or their homosexual acts in private between consenting adults; as well as anyone detained for the peaceful advocacy of the rights of homosexuals.

In carrying out this work, AI has encountered the fact that different people in different societies may not have access to places fitting a strict definition of "private." Therefore, while recognizing the internationally accepted right of a government to protect members of its society from unwanted exposure to sexual conduct, whether heterosexual or homosexual, the organization's work has included investigating cases where homosexual acts occur outside the home in places which *may* be regarded as being in private, provided sufficient safeguards are taken to conceal the sexual acts from others.

The concept of adulthood poses similar problems, so that the organization has investigated certain cases using the benchmark of 18 years of age. It will, however, consider for adoption on a case by case basis, cases where the parties are under, but close to, the age of 18.

In many cases AI's work on behalf of homosexuals may include working to urge the repeal of legislation that could result in the detention of prisoners of conscience on the basis of sexual identity.

AI opposes torture and killing by governments in all cases, and takes action against deliberate and arbitrary killings, torture, and hostage-taking by armed opposition groups. Any torture or killing—legally sanctioned, as in the laws of Iran, or extrajudicially, as in Colombia—of persons because of their sexual orientation is opposed by AI.

AI works to oppose the cruel, inhuman or degrading treatment of persons in detention in any situation, including that treatment based on sexual identity. In addition, AI's opposition to forcible "medical" treatment of those in custody to change sexual orientation is considered to be part of the organization's work to oppose torture, cruel, inhuman and degrading treatment.

The organization's work on behalf of persons seeking political asylum stems from its goal to protect people from arbitrary detention, torture, killing and "disappearance." If a person were to be sent back to a country where he or she might face one of these abuses, AI would act to prevent this; AI presses for asylum-seekers to have access to a fair hearing in the country in which they request asylum. AI bases this work in part on the right of all persons, elaborated in the UDHR Article 14, to seek political asylum, without discrimination or other barriers. In this context, AI would work to prevent the return—*refoulement*—of persons fleeing their homeland who are being persecuted (threats of death, torture, or imprisonment for example) because of their sexual orientation. Additionally, AI would oppose any barriers erected in asylum determination procedures in law or in practice, against persons solely because of their sexual orientation.

As AI works to ensure fair trials for political prisoners, the use of a person's status as a lesbian or gay man in an attempt to bias the judge or jury against them, or as a cover charge penalizing their internationally protected right to political participation, would be considered cause for concern.

AI is also concerned about unfair trials on criminal charges where the accused faces the death penalty. The organization has been concerned, for example that allegations of homosexuality may be used in ways that are likely to prejudice judge(s). For example, the organization noted with concern a death penalty case in the state of Georgia, USA, where allegations concerning the female juvenile defendant's practice of homosexual sexual acts were presented to the jury in inflammatory ways that the organization believes may have impermissibly contributed to her sentence of death (since reversed; see section on the death penalty).

Supporting the work of others for dignity and basic rights: a part of the evolving international human rights movement.

In all areas of its mandate, AI can and will work directly on individual cases. The organization will also take action that supports the ability of other human rights groups to work more effectively—including the many different domestic and international groups that have begun to document abuses against lesbians and gay men. AI's recent experience in taking up cases of lesbians and gay men as prisoners of conscience has put the organization in touch with the wide range and growing number of organizations in this field.

Additionally, in beginning to do this work, AI has entered into the public discussion on the ways in which the struggle for the human rights of lesbians and gay men is part of the on-going debates on universality of human rights and multi-culturalism.

Just as with all of our work, we are part of an evolving process. The way governments respond to the many different ways people choose to express their identification needs further examination.

Recognition of the basic dignity of all people is at the core of human rights law. Though there is international agreement that every human being has claims upon their government, arising simply as a matter of their common humanity, recognition of lesbians and gay men (as members of a particular group) has not been explicitly enumerated in existing international human rights treaties.

Lesbians and gay men were among the groups persecuted during the Second World War. Yet, while much of the impetus behind the evolution of international human rights law as it exists today emerged in reaction to the atrocities committed at that time, lesbians and gay men have generally been left out of the framework of international human rights protection. Recently, however, some steps have been taken at local and regional levels to protect gay men and lesbians through the human rights law of privacy and non-discrimination.

"The defense of human rights of homosexuals [solely] by homosexuals is impossible - or at best, [places them] in imminent peril of their lives. The struggle must be taken up by outsiders, gay or straight people, who are not themselves the victims of this hostile society. While our primary concern may be lesbian and gay people branded as 'desechables'-'disposables,' sexual orientation is only one of many reasons why people are so stigmatized. Those who oppress and kill "disposables" do not trouble themselves to treat them in discrete categories...it is absolutely crucial for gay and lesbian rights groups to make coalitions with diverse, broad-based human rights organizations to accomplish the hoped for goal... if those more diverse groups are genuinely committed to the essential principles of human dignity and rights, they should welcome a call for solidarity from their gay and lesbian comrades."[4]

Juan Pablo Ordonez
Colombian Human Rights Activist

The principle of non-discrimination is at the heart of each of the major human rights instruments. However, discrimination against lesbians and gay men is often the basis for violations of a broad range of their rights, including the right to liberty and security of the person, restrictions on freedom of movement, freedom of conscience, expression, association and assembly and the right to be free from cruel, inhuman or degrading treatment or punishment (as well as equal protection under the law). Such violations of fundamental civil and political rights often go in tandem with deprivation of the rights of lesbians and gay men to economic, social and cultural rights, such as the right to work, the right to education, the right to housing, the right to social security, or the right to health. Though Amnesty International restricts its work largely to the protection of those in custody and those threatened with deliberate and arbitrary killing, the organization recognizes that economic, social and cultural rights are inextricably intertwined with civil and political rights.

The idea that the state should not unjustifiably intrude into the personal lives of its citizens, especially in matters of such fundamental importance to human happiness as who and how one chooses to love, has generally been protected under the right to privacy. A right to privacy can be found in local, national, regional, and international legal instruments. Recognition of this right has been used nationally and regionally to force the repeal of laws that criminalize sexual activity between adults of the same sex.

International law and standards are not only made at the international level, but at the regional level as well. Regional inter-governmental organizations exist in Europe, Africa, and the Americas. In three major rulings by the European Court of Human Rights, laws which criminalized private homosexual acts in the United Kingdom, Ireland, and Cyprus were found to violate the right to a private life. Decisions in Dudgeon v. United Kingdom; Norris v. Ireland; and Modinos v. Cyprus establish important legal steps toward greater protection of the lives of lesbians and gay men.

The age at which one is permitted by national law to engage in sexual activity is set by age of consent laws. There is no universal age of consent for sexual activity whether homosexual or heterosexual. National and local age of consent laws may reflect gender and sexual identity biases. For example, many places set a higher age of consent for homosexual sexual activity than for heterosexual activity. While AI agrees that governments have the right to determine age of consent, the organization is concerned that age of consent laws not be used in an unjustifiably discriminatory way to imprison lesbians and gay men.

2 Human Rights Abuses Based on Sexual Orientation

Many governments violate the human rights of their citizens. Unfair trials, torture (including rape), cruel and degrading practices, and even murder are used by authorities to intimidate and control. There is ample evidence that governments in all regions of the world direct abuse specifically at homosexuals.

The violations lesbians and gay men face range from subtle discrimination and everyday hostility by agents of government to outright imprisonment, torture, and execution. Lesbians and gay men face both classic violations of their human rights and specifically tailored abuses, such as practices aimed at forcibly "changing" their sexual orientation.

No experience is representative: each victim suffers uniquely. But Amnesty International has found that those suffering abuse for their real or perceived homosexuality do suffer common experiences and that the stigmatized position of gays around the world contributes to their experiences of ill-treatment at the hands of authorities.

Extrajudicial executions and "disappearances"

"Disappearances" and extrajudicial executions take place at the hands of government authorities and those working with them. In some countries paramilitary groups or "death squads" violate human rights as covert arms of the state, with official approval. Wherever they operate, authorities claim to be unable to control such groups, and refuse to accept responsibility for bringing these abuses to an end.

"Death squads" and the full range of government and semi-official units that carry out extrajudicial executions and "disappearances" are often present in countries that are undergoing extreme civil unrest. Often, however, waves of extrajudicial executions occur outside any context of conflict when public authorities join with private interests to physically eliminate those they consider troublesome. They may target political opponents of the government in power, members of racial or ethnic minorities, or social "undesirables." When lesbians and gay men are targeted in such operations, they are at high risk, with little or no social or political support available to expose, denounce or stop the abuses. The consequences of speaking out may be as bad or worse than keeping quiet: in one case, a bisexual man in Brazil was tortured and killed after seeking official protection from his would-be assassins.

International standards prohibit extrajudicial executions: the deliberate and unlawful killing of persons, either by or with the consent of government authority. "Disappearances" violate many different rights, as prisoners vanish into secret cells without even an acknowledgement that they have been detained, that they are alive, that they will ever be seen again. Human rights activists have been obliged to prove wrong, against enormous odds, the jailers' refrain to the prisoner that "no one knows you are here"; that "no one knows you're even alive."

Because many lesbians and gay men experience difficulty in claiming their rights under the law, the abuses committed against them are even more difficult to monitor and punish. In Colombia, hundreds of killings of so-called "social undesirables" have been reported in urban areas, although it is only recently that these killings have come fully onto the domestic human rights agenda. The victims have been largely "invisible." This form of what Colombians have termed "social cleansing" includes homosexuals among its targets (along with vagrants and petty criminals). Victims of these "death squads" are gunned down in the streets at night or seized and driven away in unmarked cars.

Their bodies, which are rarely identified, often bear signs of torture. The perpetrators of these acts have frequently been identified as members of the National Police.

In Brazil, on the evening of March 14, 1993, Renildo José dos Santos, a bisexual local Councilor, was violently abducted from his home in Coqueiro Sêco, in Alagoas State of Northeastern Brazil, by a group of unidentified heavily armed men. Relatives of Renildo José dos Santos who witnessed the abduction believe that some of the men were plain clothes police officers. Dos Santos' headless body was found two days later in an area of waste ground bearing the marks of torture.

Dos Santos had repeatedly denounced death threats which he had received since 1989 from the local mayor and the mayor's father, also a political leader. He also accused a local police officer of making an attempt on his life. According to written testimony which he made in September 1991, he reported the death threats to a local judge but no steps were reportedly taken to ensure his physical safety. On November 27, 1991, dos Santos was shot and wounded three times, allegedly by a local police officer whom he named in his testimony. Renildo José dos Santos attributed the death threats and the attempt against his life to political differences with the mayor and his father, and to his bisexuality, which he had publicly acknowledged on a radio program. He claimed that the local police had not conducted a proper investigation into the attempt against his life, and that the local police officer had not been suspended from duty pending the outcome of the investigation.

In January 1993, the local Council of Coqueiro Sêco set up a parliamentary commission of inquiry to investigate the conduct of Councilor dos Santos under accusations that he had committed acts "incompatible with Parliamentary decorum," i.e. homosexual acts. As a result of the inquiry, dos Santos was stripped of his local Council seat by the Council. He was subsequently reinstated, pending a judicial appeal.

On February 25, several local human rights organizations wrote to the State Secretary for Public Security denouncing the death threats and the alleged involvement of military police officers in the attempts on dos Santos' life. To Amnesty International's knowledge, no protection was granted to Councilor dos Santos.

In a statement to the newspaper Jornal de Alagoas a few days before his assassination, Councilor dos Santos reiterated his denunciations of death threats and discrimination against him, and attributed the smear campaign to his public acknowledgment of his bisexuality. He said that he was frightened and desperate and that he feared a new attempt on his life or an abduction.

Those who come to the aid of homosexual human rights victims are sometimes targeted themselves. Following the killing of Councilor dos Santos, Reinaldo Cabral, a correspondent for a Rio de Janeiro newspaper *Jornal do Brasil*, wrote an article denouncing police violence and the threats of continued violence against two of dos Santos' relatives. In the early hours of the morning of 8 April two unknown persons entered the front garden of Cabral's home, and while one of them held a gun, the other poured petrol over Cabral's car and set it on fire before fleeing.

Torture and ill-treatment

Torture is any act by which severe pain or suffering, whether physical or mental, is intentionally inflicted for any purpose such as punishment, obtaining information, intimidation, coercion or for any reason, when such pain or suffering is inflicted either by or with the acquiescence of a public official. Torture and ill-treatment are used by many governments around the world to suppress dissent, intimidate political activists, and threaten certain sectors of the population. Lesbians and gay men in the custody of government officials often face torture and ill-treatment. In some countries, homosexual activists are targeted as "examples," in attempts to control their public identities and community activism, while in other places gay people living relatively quiet and private lives may fall victim to this type of government abuse.

Torture or ill-treatment are sometimes used to force "confessions" of homosexuality, or to elicit the names and addresses of other lesbians and gay men. Lesbians and gay men who face torture and ill-treatment may be doubly victimized, as societal discrimination prevents them from seeking the legal, religious, social, or psychiatric support services available to other victims. Often these abuses are kept secret, rendering the wounds even more difficult to heal.

In Romania, gay men have been routinely targeted for ill-treatment and torture. Doru Marian Beldie, 19 years old, was arrested in Bucharest in June 1992 for allegedly having sex with a minor. Beldie was beaten with truncheons on the palms of his hands and soles of his feet for several hours in order to force him to sign a confession. Currently serving a sentence of four years and six months under Article 200, which allows for the imprisonment of men who have engaged in consensual adult homosexual relations, Doru Marian Beldie has allegedly been raped repeatedly by other prisoners.

In another case, Marcel Brosca, a 20-year-old student, was beaten and ill-treated by police officers until he signed a confession. According to the report received by Amnesty International, at the time of his arrest Marcel Brosca was commuting by train from Galati where he studied to his native village when he overslept and woke up in Tecuci. As there was no train back that same evening he went to sleep in the station waiting room. He was reportedly awakened by four policemen accompanied by a 17-year-old boy. Pointing to Marcel the policemen asked the boy if this was the man for whom they had been searching and the boy responded affirmatively.

Marcel Brosca was beaten for three or four hours after being detained by the police; he was then pulled by the hair, the sides and back of his head were beaten against the table and the wall until blood poured over his face, his arms were twisted, and he was beaten on the soles of his feet with truncheons.

Ienel S., aged 21, was arrested in October 1990 after having been accused of forcing another man to have oral sex with him. He was reportedly beaten by police officers from 7 am to 8 pm. They beat him with wooden sticks on the torso and on the back, as well as on the hands and feet in order to force him to sign a confession. After signing this confession, he was reportedly taken in a semi-conscious state to a doctor to be examined. Without a proper investigation, the doctor signed a certificate which made no mention of his injuries.

According to the information received by Amnesty International, it seems unlikely that Ienel S. used force in connection with the sexual acts for which he is charged, and it also seems likely that Ienel S. was reported to the police by a police informant. Ienel S. was eligible for parole on 22 September 1993. Regardless of his possible release from prison, AI will continue to press for a full and impartial investigation of allegations that he was ill-treated following his arrest.

Allegations of ill-treatment of homosexuals by police in Britain were made to Amnesty International by people who believe the abuse was directed at them because of their homosexual identity and/or their racial or ethnic group affiliation. Some of these complainants have been awarded civil damages.

Complaints of ill-treatment have also been received by AI regarding police officers in Los Angeles, California, USA. Robert Cervantes, a gay Latino, was beaten by two Los Angeles Police Department officers in an adult cinema during an arrest on suspicion of lewd conduct. Cervantes alleged that two police officers pounced on him before he reached his seat, striking him in the face with their metal badges and generally assaulting him. He also alleged that he was hit on the head with a sap while handcuffed in the back of the officers' vehicle. Cervantes was later acquitted on criminal charges of lewd conduct, battery of police officers, and resisting arrest. In a subsequent trial, the two arresting officers were found guilty of using excessive force, and Cervantes was awarded punitive damages.

International laws against torture include government obligations to prevent, investigate, prosecute, and punish the torturer and compensate the victim. The state bears responsibility for government agents who participate or acquiesce in the torture of lesbians or gay men in their custody. Failure of a government to prosecute its own agents or to provide an effective system of investigation and redress for private acts of violence against lesbians and gay men violates their rights under international human rights treaties. Fear of violence further impairs the ability of homosexuals to exercise their other internationally protected rights.

In Turkey, although homosexuality is not illegal, gay rights activists have been subjected to harassment, intimidation, and ill-treatment. In recent years, homosexuals and transvestites, in Istanbul in particular, have begun to publicly address these problems. Some have spoken nationally and internationally on behalf of those marginalized in Turkish society. Transvestites in Istanbul are concentrated in Cihangir, a part of Beyoğlu district, and have frequently complained about harassment by the police.

On the night of 10 August 1991, the houses of several transvestites in Istanbul were raided by the local police. Six people were detained including Ramazan (Demet) Demir, a member of the Istanbul Human Rights Association and a gay rights activist. Upon his release six days later, Ramazan (Demet) Demir alleged that he had been severely beaten with a length of a rubber-covered steel hose by the Chief of Police at Beyoğlu Police Station and obtained a medical report from the Forensic Medical Institute certifying that he had injuries consistent with his allegations. After publicly protesting his torture, he was again detained and finally charged with "insulting the memory of Mustafa Kemal Atatürk," after he pointed out to the arresting officers that homosexuality was not proscribed by the laws which had been introduced by Atatürk.

Amnesty International has received information that at least seven transvestites were reportedly arrested by police agents in San José, Costa Rica in 1993. They were held for several hours and subjected to torture or cruel, inhuman or degrading treatment. At least one of these men was subjected to mockery and sexual abuse.

Greek newspapers periodically report cases of police officers torturing or ill-treating homosexuals who are randomly detained during operations aimed at clearing areas of homosexuals, drug users, or following political or social demonstrations.

Rape and sexual abuse

Amnesty International considers the rape of persons in detention as a form of torture. UN experts have also defined rape as a method of torture, including the insertion of objects into the orifices of the body. For example, the UN's Special Rapporteur on Torture has said that because rape and other forms of sexual assault were clearly "...a particularly ignominious violation of the inherent dignity and right to physical integrity of the human being, they accordingly constituted an act of torture."[5] Further compounding the violation, domestic judicial and legislative remedies are often not available to lesbians and gay men who have been raped in detention because of ostracism, fear, or loss of family support.

In some countries, rape and sexual abuse by government officials is a common method of torture inflicted on female detainees. Amnesty has received reports that this method of torture is also sometimes used against men, including gay men. Rape is both a physical assault and injury, as well as an assault on the victim's mental and emotional well-being. Interrogators and other government officials may use rape and sexual abuse as a form of torture to force "confessions" of homosexuality, or use these rapes as "proof" that the detainee is gay or lesbian. Homosexuals who have been raped may be afraid to report these abuses, because the very act could be seen, contradictorily, to confirm the suspicions of the detainee's homosexuality.

In April, 1993, in San José, Costa Rica, several transvestites were arrested and subjected to degrading sexual abuse. One of them, Manuel Horacio Guevara Albornoz, was reportedly arrested wearing women's clothes. He was taken to the radio patrol unit, where policemen reportedly mocked and fondled him.

He was re-arrested in May, taken to the same radio patrol unit, made to strip, and subjected to further mockery.

José Enrique Vargas Gonzalez was arrested in May by two policemen, driven to the ruins of a house, and reportedly forced at gunpoint to have oral sex with one of the officers. Investigations into these cases were carried out by the Costa Rican Ministry of the Interior.

Forced "medical" treatment to change sexual orientation

In some countries, lesbians and gay men in custody have been subjected to forced "medical" treatment to change their sexual orientation. This kind of abuse may include electric shock and other forms of "aversion therapy" or the use of psychotropic drugs.

In 1982, Amnesty International condemned "medical" treatment carried out on people in detention against their will for the purpose of altering their sexual orientation. Reports of this kind of ill-treatment have been received by Amnesty International regarding practices in the former Soviet Union and in China.

Imprisonment

Many countries have laws that enable officials to imprison gay men and lesbians for advocacy of homosexual equality and/or for consensual sexual acts in private between adults. These laws are sometimes said to protect society from "immoral" or "unnatural" acts. Under these laws it becomes illegal to be gay or lesbian: sexual orientation is an integral part of a person's identity, and the threat of detention impinges on a gay person's entire life.

Detention for the advocacy of homosexual rights

In addition to legislation which proscribes homosexual acts, laws regarding public behavior and morality may be used to target lesbians and gay men. In Greece, Irene Petropoulu, the chief editor of the gay and lesbian magazine *Amphi,* was sentenced to five months' imprisonment and a 50,000 drachmas fine on charges of violating Articles 29, 30, and 31 of Law 5060/1931 for a comment she published in an issue of the magazine in 1991. The comment, in the classified section, asked why so many homosexual and heterosexual men were interested in corresponding with lesbians. The court ruled that the comment "offends public feelings of decency and sexual morals and cannot be considered to be a work of art and science." Irene Petropoulou is free pending appeal. If her appeal is unsuccessful, she will face a term of imprisonment. Amnesty International has expressed concern about Petropoulou's sentence, and will consider her to be a prisoner of conscience if she is imprisoned.

In Mexico, two gay activists and AIDS prevention workers were arrested in 1992. On 16 June members of the federal judicial police arrested Gerardo Rubén Ortega Zurita and José Cruz Reyes Potenciano, both renowned in Mexico City for their AIDS-prevention voluntary work among male prostitutes in that city. Each man was accused of the rape and sexual assault of a minor. They were both transferred to a police station, where the police announced their arrest to the press, despite the lack, at the time, of formal charges against the defendants. Both were reportedly beaten by the police and transferred the same day to another police station, where they remained incommunicado until the next day.

On 17 June formal charges were brought. Medical examinations carried out on the day of arrest on both men reportedly certified that the injuries of the defendants were consistent with the allegations of beatings by the police. Two days later, the two men were transferred to a prison in Mexico City, pending trial. On the days following their arrival, both reportedly suffered beatings and harassment from other prison inmates. On 31 March 1993, they were both sentenced to 13 years and nine months' imprisonment.

Amnesty International appealed on behalf of the two men in June 1993, expressing concern to Mexican authorities that their arrests may have been motivated by their active campaigning on gay issues in the capital, including their outspoken criticism of alleged police abuse of homosexuals. It called for an inquiry into the alleged abuse of the two men who, it said, appeared to be prisoners of conscience, held solely for their advocacy of the rights of members of Mexico's gay community. On 9 July 1993, the two men were released following a successful appeal, cleared of all charges.

In Turkey, following the suicide of a transvestite in Istanbul, several transvestites held a press conference on 7 December 1989 at the Yeni Bizans (New Byzantine) Cultural Center, owned by Ibrahim Eren. That evening Ibrahim Eren was arrested and charged with violating Law No. 2911 on Demonstrations and Assembly under Article 536 of the Turkish Penal Code, "the illegal distribution of leaflets in public places". He was committed to Bayrampaşa Prison in Istanbul. Two other activists, Ahmet Oğuz Akdoğan and Aydin Menteşe, were indicted along with Ibrahim Eren, but not imprisoned pending trial.

Twenty-eight foreign and three Turkish gay activists were detained in July 1993 also in Istanbul, solely by reason of advocacy of homosexual equality and their sexual orientation. The first Congress of Homosexual Solidarity was to be held in Istanbul during the weekend of 2-6 July 1993. However, after receiving initial permission from the Interior Minister, the Congress was reportedly banned at the last minute by the Governor of Istanbul on the grounds that it would be contrary to the "traditions and moral values" of Turkish society and might disturb the peace. On 3 July, delegates who were planning to attend the Congress decided to hold a press conference to protest the ban. Three Turkish activists, Huseyin Kuşkaya, Cem Özipek and Onur Sarvaut, were arrested before the press conference, the majority

> ***Lesbian and gay activists are often involved in other human rights struggles in their countries. Black gay and anti-apartheid activist Simon Tseko Nkoli was detained by South African authorities along with a number of others and charged with treason. The so-called Delmas Treason Trial which began in January 1986 ended with his acquittal. According to Nkoli, "In South Africa all issues are linked together. Homophobia is part of discrimination. We can not deal with it in isolation. We are trying to link our struggle with the struggle of the majority of the people against apartheid and racism." All Delmas prisoners had been released by December 1989 after international appeals on their behalf.***

of the foreign delegates were detained on their way to the press conference, and the remaining delegates were detained at their hotel.

Police initially took the foreign delegates to a local police station and said they would be strip searched. When they protested, this was not carried out. They were held in a police bus for most of the day, until other delegates had been brought from their hotel. They were then taken to Istanbul airport to be deported that same evening. However, en route to the airport, the police bus turned off the airport road and took the detainees to a local hospital where the delegates were told they would have to submit to a blood test for the HIV virus. The delegates refused to permit blood to be drawn and the authorities ultimately withdrew their demand. Finally, they were deported to Germany. The sole motivation of the attempts to submit the detainees to strip searches and blood tests appears to have been to punish or humiliate them for their homosexuality and gay rights advocacy.

Detention for homosexual identity or homosexual acts

Lesbians and gay men have historically been persecuted and oppressed through laws that criminalize sexual behavior between consenting adults of the same sex, even when such behavior occurs in private. While the language of these laws varies with regard to the specific acts which are proscribed, the common effect is to stigmatize lesbians and gay men as criminals. While these laws are not always used by authorities to imprison lesbians and gay men, in many cases their existence provides the context for discrimination and violence against homosexuals.

In Australia, certain sections of the Criminal Code of the State of Tasmania criminalize all homosexual acts between consenting men in private. Although other states in Australia have acted to decriminalize homosexual acts, Tasmania has not. In December of 1991, a gay rights activist from Hobart, Tasmania filed a complaint with the United Nations Human Rights Committee charging that the anti-sodomy laws in Tasmania violated his human rights. At the time of publication of this report, this petition is still pending. Amnesty International has repeatedly called for the repeal of such laws.

Vladimir Mironov, aged 43, was arrested on 11 October 1990 and charged under Article 121 part 1 of the Russian Federation Criminal Code, which punished consenting sexual acts between adult males. He stood trial in May 1991, when he and at least one witness are said to have retracted testimony given during the investigation on the grounds that it had been extracted under physical duress. He was sentenced to three years' imprisonment by the Volgograd District People's Court in Moscow, but following an appeal Moscow City Court ordered a reinvestigation of the case.

Vladimir Mironov's appeal was heard on 17 March 1992. Although he and his partner admitted having sexual relations, they denied having anal intercourse (only this form was punishable under the Russian Article 121), and the case was closed in the absence of a corpus delicti. The Court also accepted the allegations by witnesses questioned during the preliminary investigation that testimony had been obtained from them by police using threats.

Several former Soviet republics have decriminalized consensual homosexual activity between adults in private, including Estonia, Latvia, Lithuania, Ukraine, and Russia. In Latvia, the Minister of Justice told Amnesty International that all "persons who had been punished for homosexuality were immediately released from punishment after the adoption of the [new] legislation." In other countries that have amended their laws, prisoners may remain.

Many former Soviet republics have retained their sodomy laws. In Uzbekistan, Article 100 of the Criminal Code, which punishes consenting homosexual activity between men, was still being applied as of early 1993. According to the Justice Minister of Uzbekistan, a small number of men have been convicted under this article since the republic gained independence. Amnesty International has expressed concern about the continuing existence of laws criminalizing consensual homosexual acts between adult men in the former Soviet republics of Belarus, Georgia, Kazakhstan, and Kyrgyzstan. It is unclear how many people are being held in jail under these laws.

In many countries where laws against homosexual behavior are in force, lesbians and gay men are often jailed with little or no evidence of having engaged in sexual acts, underlining the function of these laws as public regulators of gay identity.

In Romania, two gay men who had been living together, Mirel Ciprian Cucu and Milorad Mutascu, were arrested in January 1993 and placed in preventative detention. Mirel Cucu was charged under Article 200, paragraph 1, of the Romanian Penal Code and faced a possible prison sentence of one to five years for "having sexual relations with a person of the same sex." He was released after two months' detention. Milorad Mutascu was charged under the same article, paragraph 2, for homosexual relations with a minor and faced a possible prison sentence of two to seven years. (Romanian law punishes sexual relations between men at any age; a heterosexual relationship between people of the same ages as Cucu and Mutascu would have been lawful). In April, Amnesty International called for the immediate release of Milorad Mutascu from prison. The Timisoara court released him on 12 May 1993.

Mirel Ciprian Cucu and Milorad Mutascu were tried by the County Court of Timisoara on 9 June 1993. They received suspended sentences of one and two years imprisonment, respectively. In addition to their time in jail, the two men also faced vilification in the official police newspaper, Tim-polis, which published their names, photos, and addresses even before formal charges were brought against them. The paper described their relationship as a "social danger," disregarding their well-being and slandering their reputations in a homophobic society.

Amnesty International is also concerned that Romanian authorities have sentenced three men, Marius Aitai, Cosmin Hutanu, and Ovidiu Chetea, to up to two-and-a-half years' imprisonment solely for practicing homosexual acts in private. The three men were among 57 people detained in Romanian prisons on 18 November 1993 who had been convicted under Article 200. AI considers Aitai, Hutanu, and Ovidiu to be prisoners of conscience and called for their immediate and unconditional release.

In June 1992, the Nicaraguan government approved amending Article 205 of its Penal Code to provide that "anyone who induces, promotes, propagandizes or practices in scandalous form sexual intercourse between persons of the same sex commits the crime of sodomy and shall incur one to three years' imprisonment." The amendment of Article 205 could allow for imprisonment of adults who engage in consensual homosexual conduct in private; these people would be considered by AI to be prisoners of conscience. In addition, this amended Article includes a broad, undefined provision criminalizing homosexual acts practiced "in scandalous form." Amnesty International is also concerned that those involved in the non-violent advocacy of homosexual rights who could be considered to be "promoting" homosexual acts and

Renildo José Dos Santos
Bisexual City Councillor killed in Algaoas, Brazil in March 1993.

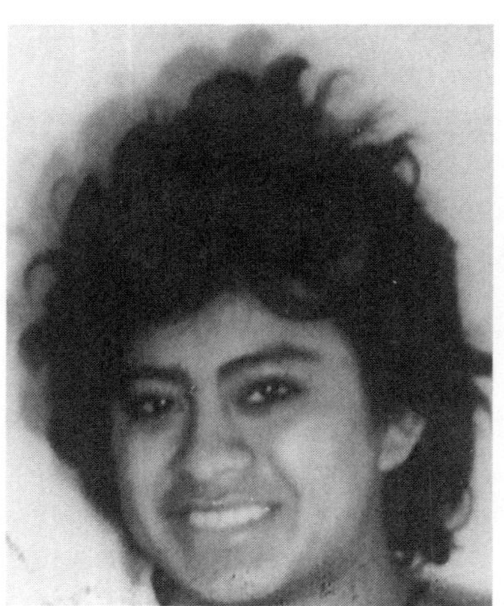

José Reyes Potenciano and Gerardo Ortega Zurita
Mexican gay rights activists renowned for their voluntary AIDS prevention work among male prostitutes in Mexico City. They were detained and beaten by police while being held incommunicado and were charged with the rape and sexual assault of a minor. AI took up their cases in June 1993. They appealed in July 1993 and were released after being cleared of all charges.

Doru Marian Beldie, 19 years of age
Arrested July 1992 and convicted under Article 200 of the Romanian Penal Code. Currently incarcerated at Jilava Prison.

Milorad Mutascu, age 22, arrested along with his roommate, Mirel Ciprian Cucu. Both were placed in preventive detention and charged under Article 200 of the Romanian Penal Code. Cucu was released after 2 months. AI took up Mutascu's case in April 1993, calling for his immediate release. Mutascu and Cucu were tried in June 1993 and received suspended sentences.

AIUSA Local Group 23 petition table at
Munchies Cafe, Houston TX, December 1993.

AIUSA members participate in the April 25, 1993 March on Washington for Lesbian, Gay, and Bi Equal Rights

Black gay and anti-apartheid activist, Simon Tseko Nkoli with former New York City Mayor David Dinkins and representatives of that city's people of color gay and lesbian community.

would therefore be eligible for punishment under this law.

In the United Kingdom territory of the Isle of Man and in Ireland, laws criminalizing consensual sex between adult men were repealed in 1992 and 1993, respectively.

Twenty-eight of the fifty United States have repealed their criminal sodomy statutes since 1962; while other statutes are still being challenged. Five states (Arkansas, Kansas, Missouri, Montana, Tennessee) apply these laws only to homosexuals. Amnesty International would consider persons imprisoned under these laws as a prisoner of conscience.

Even where prosecutions are rarely reported, the criminalization of gay and lesbian relationships can provide a permanent source of anxiety to gay men and lesbians by holding over them a constant threat of prosecution. It can also figure in civil proceedings even when no criminal charges have been brought. For example, in 1993, a Virginia court denied Sharon Bottoms, a lesbian, custody of her two-year old son. It is reported that the court referred to the state's criminal sodomy statute in declaring her an "unfit parent."

These state laws have been upheld by the U.S. Supreme Court: in the 1986 case of Bowers v. Hardwick, the Court upheld the constitutionality of Georgia's criminal sodomy statute, stating that the U.S. Constitution does not guarantee a "fundamental right to homosexuals to engage in acts of consensual sodomy." However, in 1992 the Kentucky Supreme Court in Commonwealth v. Wasson found that the state's criminal sodomy law violated the "right to privacy" embodied in the Kentucky state constitution, and denied equal protection of the law to homosexuals.

Although in some countries homosexuality is not specifically criminalized, the absence of these laws does not necessarily safeguard the basic human rights of lesbians and gays. People continue to be harassed and arbitrarily detained solely by reason of their sexual orientation. In many places, people suspected of homosexual behavior are detained on ambiguous criminal charges ranging from vagrancy to "hooliganism," or detained without charge or trial under systems of administrative detention.

In China, prior to November 1992, homosexuals were harassed by the police and sent to "re-education through labor camps." Some were also reportedly sentenced to terms of imprisonment under criminal laws such as "disturbing social order" and "hooliganism." A Canton newspaper reported in February 1992 that a man was sentenced to eight years in jail for having homosexual relations with other men. In another case, two lesbians who had been living together in Anhui province were detained for 15 days on charges of "unruly behavior" while the case was referred to a higher authority. In April 1992, the Ministry of Public Security decided to release the women, finding that there was no legal basis on which to prosecute them.

Provisions against homosexuality in criminal law were reportedly repealed in 1992. Reports indicate that in November of that year, the Communist Party declared that it no longer regarded homosexuality as an offense, and provincial police departments were instructed not to arrest homosexuals. Current policies on the treatment of lesbians and gay men are unclear and vary from region to region. Despite the 1992 change in law, Amnesty has received reports of some quite recent cases in which people have been imprisoned in connection with their homosexuality.

Arrests and detentions of gays simply because they are gay continue to be reported from many parts of the world. Over the last two years, such arrests have been reported in the Bahamas, Romania, Russia, Turkey, and Mexico. Arbitrary detention of transvestites and gay men has also been reported in Costa Rica where, on 6 February 1993, over 10 people were detained in a police raid on a gay bar. Frequent raids on gay bars occurred in Costa Rica in the mid-1980s, but appear to have stopped.

Inadequate or unfair legal proceedings

Each year unfair trials violate the fundamental rights of political prisoners throughout the world. International instruments, including the Universal Declaration of Human Rights and the International Covenant on Civil and Political Rights, guarantee the right to a fair, prompt, and public hearing by an independent and impartial tribunal. The specific internationally recognized requirements for legal proceedings are set forth in the International Covenant on Civil and Political Rights and other instruments.

AI's work for prisoners of conscience includes work for the release of anyone imprisoned solely for their actual or alleged homosexuality, as well as anyone facing detention for their peaceful advocacy of the rights of homosexuals. In AI's work for fair trials for all political prisoners, it sometimes finds that a person's real or alleged sexual orientation may result in unfair trials. Sometimes charges founded on allegations of homosexual behavior will also be used by governments as a pretext to discredit critics, as in Iran where a Sunni religious leader was executed after the government said he had "confessed" to spying, adultery, and sodomy.

AI is also concerned about unfair trials on criminal charges where the accused faces the death penalty as allegations of homosexuality may be impermissably accepted by judge or jury as factors relevant to the culpability of the accused. For example, in the United States, Janice Buttrum was convicted of murder and sentenced to death when she was 18 years old. She was 17 years old at the time of the crime. By the time of the trial, much publicity had been generated in the local press regarding the crime. Janice Buttrum was repeatedly described as a bisexual sadist. The defense asked for a change of trial venue, which was not granted. During the sentencing hearing, a private psychologist appeared as a witness for the state. Although he had not interviewed Janice Buttrum in person, he testified that she was a sexual sadist, and said that she would commit other violent sexual acts in the future (Janice Buttrum had only one previous conviction for a minor offense, not involving sexual violence). She was sentenced to death in 1981. Following appeals, this decision was vacated and Buttrum was sentenced to life imprisonment on the grounds that she had not received a fair sentencing hearing.

The death penalty

International human rights standards recognize each person's right not to be arbitrarily deprived of their life and categorically state that no one shall be subjected to torture or to cruel, inhuman, or degrading treatment or punishment. The UN has committed itself to the gradual abolition of the death penalty. Amnesty International opposes the death penalty in all circumstances, and also points out when it is used in a discriminatory manner, such as against persons based on their sexual, racial, or ethnic identity.

Although referred to as a "punishment" for crime, the death penalty is often arbitrary, used as a tool for political repression or disproportionately imposed on the poor and powerless. Like other disenfranchised groups, lesbians and gay men sometimes face the death penalty for their identity, including their homosexual conduct.

In Iran, sodomy is punishable by death. During 1992 at least 330 people were executed in Iran. It is unclear how many of these executions may have resulted from accusations of homosexuality. Although Amnesty International has received reports that some lesbians and gay men have been stoned to death or beheaded for their homosexuality, it has been extremely difficult to substantiate these reports. What is clear is that homosexuality is a capital crime in Iran. In July 1980, a 38-year-old man, married with six children, was stoned to death in the town of Kerman in southern Iran. He had been convicted of homosexuality and adultery.

In at least one case, homosexuality was used as one of the pretexts for application of the death penalty. Dr. Ali Mozaffarian, a well-known surgeon and one of the leaders of the Sunni Muslim community in Fars province in southern Iran, was executed in Shiraz in early August 1992. He was convicted of spying for the United States and Iraq, as well as adultery and sodomy. His videotaped "confessions," which may have been obtained as a result of physical or psychological pressure, were broadcast on television. Amnesty International believes that his trial may have been unfair, and that the charges of spying, adultery, and homosexuality were merely used to target this Sunni Muslim leader.

In other countries where *hadd* offenses (offenses against divine will under Shari'a or Islamic law) are in effect, homosexuality is often punishable by death. In Mauritania, the 1983 Penal Code introduced homosexuality as a *hadd* offense, prescribing the death penalty for Muslims convicted of homosexuality. In the Arab Republic of Yemen, sodomy is specified as a *hadd* offense, punishable by execution. In other countries where Shari'a is the basis for penal codes, lesbians and gay men may be vulnerable to human rights abuses. Although sodomy and homosexuality may not be mentioned, many of these penal codes criminalize a wide range of sexual behavior outside of marriage. Countries which have such laws include Saudi Arabia, Pakistan, the Sudan, and Oman.

Abuses based on real or perceived HIV status

The incorrect linkage of HIV status and homosexual identity has resulted in increased discrimination and abuse aimed at homosexuals. Gay men are often considered to be "AIDS carriers," and as a result may be subjected to ill-treatment at the hands of government authorities. In addition, activists who are working to prevent the spread of the AIDS virus in gay communities may be targeted for human rights abuses.

In Nicaragua, AIDS activists are believed to be vulnerable to charges under an anti-sodomy law signed into effect in 1992. The law states that "anyone who induces, promotes, propagandizes or practices in scandalous form sexual intercourse between persons of the same sex commits the crime of sodomy and shall incur 1 to 3 years imprisonment." Amnesty International is concerned that AIDS activists who provide safer sex information to lesbians and gay men may be considered to be "promoting" homosexuality, and may thus be eligible for imprisonment under this law.

In Mexico, two prominent gay activists educating the homosexual community about HIV were sentenced to imprisonment after an unfair trial. Amnesty International is concerned that this action may have been, in part, an attempt to curb their activities on behalf of the gay community.

In Turkey, when twenty-eight foreign gay activists were detained solely because of their advocacy of gay rights, they were asked to submit to a blood test for the AIDS virus. They refused to give blood, and the authorities eventually rescinded their request. These are just a few examples of how the incorrect linkage of HIV status and homosexual activity become the basis of abuse.

3
Lesbians and Gay Men in Peril

Gay and lesbian organizations have developed and evolved over time and in response to social pressure and discrimination. Organizations which promote the rights of lesbians and gay men have formed on all continents. As lesbians and gay men become more vocal around the world, their rights are increasingly at risk. Some of the countries where gay and lesbian organizations currently exist include Argentina, Brazil, Chile, Colombia, Finland, France, Ghana, Hungary, India, Indonesia, Ireland, Norway, Peru, the Philippines, Malaysia, Mexico, South Africa, Thailand, the United States, and Zimbabwe. These organizations have different goals and purposes. But all are fighting for the observance of the basic human rights of an overlooked minority. Amnesty International includes information here about the work of these organizations to show the range of work presently being done to protect the human rights of lesbians and gay men. This section is by no means comprehensive or representative; there are many more organizations than those discussed below.

Although AI seeks to investigate allegations of possible human rights violations within its mandate, it has not been able to substantiate all of the allegations mentioned below.

In North America, gay and lesbian organizations are plentiful. In Canada, gay and lesbian organizations have been fighting to have sexual orientation included in that country's federal Human Rights Act.

In the United States, lesbians and gay men are fighting for the repeal of sodomy laws in six states, and against a host of state and municipal challenges to equal rights protections. In addition, gay and lesbian organizations such as the Community United Against Violence in San Francisco are working to end anti-gay hate crimes. In addition to the domestic-focused gay rights groups that seek to protect the lives of lesbians and gay men, a number of other organizations have added international concerns to their work, such as the American Civil Liberties Union and Lambda Legal Defense's immigration and asylum project. Gay and lesbian Latino/as have organized La Red, a network that works in solidarity with organizations in Latin America. Gay Native Americans have organized to combat the double-discrimination they face as Native Americans and as homosexuals.

There are many strong gay and lesbian organizations in Latin America. In Mexico, Circulo Cultural Gay has organized protests against the recent wave of assassinations aimed at gay men. Their work has been supported by many other gay and lesbian organizations, as well as the Department of Human Rights of the Archdiocese of Mexico, which reports that over thirty gay men have been killed since June 1991, possibly with state involvement. In Peru, the Movimiento Homosexual de Lima has reported that gays have been assassinated by the MRTA, an armed insurgency group. In addition, they are working against reported police abuse of lesbians and gay men. Gay and lesbian activists in Ecuador are organizing against the reported murders of gay men by so-called "death squads," which allegedly kidnap and rape men before killing them and dumping their bodies in public areas. In Brazil, the Grupo Gay da Bahia has reported that 1200 lesbians and gay men may have been killed since 1980, many by "death squads."

In the Caribbean, gay and lesbian organizations are working in several countries. In the Dominican Republic, gays and lesbians report that they are vulnerable to harassment under laws that proscribe "offenses against morality," but several groups for lesbians and gay men have formed. One such group is the lesbian group, the Colectivo Ciguay, which works against discrimination and harassment. In Jamaica, the Gay Freedom Movement of Jamaica has been publishing a magazine since the 1970s.

In Africa, there are gay and lesbian organizations in many countries. In Zimbabwe, Gays and Lesbians of Zimbabwe (GALZ) protests the social and political discrimination that gays face there, including laws that outlaw homosexuality and widespread homophobic attitudes. In Nigeria, the Gentlemen's Alliance, a group of gay men, held the country's first gay conference in 1991, despite the presence of a law that makes homosexuality punishable with up to 14 years in prison. In Ghana, the Afro Lesbian and Gay Club works against laws that ban "unnatural carnal sex". In South Africa, the Gay and Lesbian Organization of the Witwatersrand and other gay and lesbian groups worked to ensure inclusion of civil rights protections for gays and lesbians in the country's new constitution.

Lesbians and gay men are organizing throughout Asia and the Pacific. In South Asia, lesbians and gay men have banded together to fight India's Section 377, which bans "carnal intercourse against the order of nature," and which organizers say leads to harassment of gays in India. The regional coalition working against Section 377 includes Bombay Dost, Sakhi, and Arambh of India; Action for AIDS of Singapore; F.A.C.T. of Thailand; KKLGN of Indonesia; The Library Fund from the Philippines; and the Malaysian group Pink Triangle. The Asian Lesbian Network, which met for the first time in 1990, includes lesbian groups from Bangladesh, India, Indonesia, Japan, Malaysia, Singapore, and Thailand, as well as Asian lesbian groups from the US, the UK, the Netherlands, and Australia. These groups are working to define and combat the discrimination they face in their varied cultures.

In Western Europe, there are many well-organized and developed gay and lesbian organizations. Because gay and lesbian conduct is legal in nearly all Western European states, many of these movements are targeting various forms of discrimination.

In the United Kingdom, for example, the Stonewall Group compiled a dossier in 1990 on anti-homosexual discrimination in the European Community. The list of complaints included discrimination in employment, the existence of anti-gay harassment, and problems of freedom of movement within the European Community. In Britain, three young gay men have petitioned the European Court of Human Rights charging the U.K. with discrimination because of age of consent laws, which define the age of consent for heterosexuals and lesbians as 16, and for gay men as 21.

Irish lesbian and gay groups recently scored a victory in their campaign to repeal that country's sodomy law, which provided imprisonment for consensual sex between men in private. In 1993, the Irish government published the Criminal Law Bill 1993, which repealed the law forbidding homosexual acts.

In Sweden, the lesbian and gay organization, RFSL, has assisted gay and lesbian refugees in their quest for political asylum in that country. The RFSL has been successful in a number of these cases, assisting homosexuals from the Middle East, Asia, and Latin America to receive asylum based on their membership in a persecuted group.

In Greece, the lesbian and gay group, AKOE, provides support for gays within the country, protests anti-gay acts, and networks with other Mediterranean gays. In the Netherlands, black lesbians have formed Fiida, a group which works to combat discrimination based on sexual orientation and race. Lesbians and gay men in Turkey have organized the Radical Gay Group, which works against discrimination and human rights abuses carried out by the authorities against the gay community.

In Eastern Europe, lesbian and gay organizations are growing in the wake of the political changes since the fall of the Berlin Wall. In Poland, for example, the first gay and lesbian organization, Lambda, was officially registered in February 1990. Prior to this, in 1988, Homeros Lambda, a Hungarian group, became the first officially recognized gay and lesbian organization in Eastern Europe. The group has reported on a recent wave of anti-gay violence, and has protested the maintenance of "pink lists" by the Hungarian police, which are reportedly used to track homosexuals. In Latvia, lesbians and gay men who organized the Latvian Association for Sexual Equality celebrated in 1992 when Article 124.1, which had banned consensual sex between adult men, was repealed. In Croatia, Lesbians and Gay Men in Action have set up an emergency center in Zagreb for fleeing Bosnian gays. This center provides emergency shelter, counseling, and humanitarian aid.

In the Middle East, there are very few gay and lesbian organizations. In Muslim countries, homosexuals do not generally organize themselves according to gay or lesbian identities. An organization of Persian-speaking lesbians and gay men has formed in Europe, with chapters in Sweden, England, and Germany. HOMAN works for the rights of Persian-speaking and Iranian lesbians and gay men, and is particularly concerned with recent reports of executions of lesbians and gay men in Iran. Some members of this group are gay refugees, who work to spread the word about other Iranians who have suffered at the hands of the authorities. In Israel, there are several gay and lesbian organizations. One of the most well known, the Society for the Protection of Personal Rights, works for legislation to protect lesbians and gay men.

Non-governmental organizations (NGOs) play a crucial role in the promotion and protection of human rights. International non-governmental organizations carry out independent investigations, monitor and criticize the official reports presented by states and international bodies, and publicly expose gross violations of human rights.

In recent years, specifically homosexual organizations such as the International Lesbian and Gay Association and the International Gay and Lesbian Human Rights Commission have emerged to document human rights violations against gays and lesbians and to build international bridges among homosexual groups. In 1993, the UN accepted for roster status the International Lesbian and Gay Association giving it among other things the opportunity to officially present information on human rights abuses against homosexuals to the human rights bodies.

In a hopeful trend, mainstream human rights NGOs traditionally concerned with monitoring violations are beginning to join international efforts to secure the rights of lesbians and gay men. It is hoped that these efforts by Amnesty International to publicize human rights violations based on sexual orientation will contribute to placing these violations squarely onto the agenda of human rights organizations, the United Nations, and other inter-governmental bodies.

4
Breaking the Silence: recommendations for the protection of the lives of lesbians and gay men

Amnesty International recommends that governments:

- Release all prisoners of conscience immediately and unconditionally, including all persons imprisoned for their homosexual identity, for homosexual acts in private between consenting adults, for advocating the rights of homosexuals (including in the context of HIV/AIDS education), or under the pretext of charges of homosexuality.

- Review all legislation and practices including sodomy laws (and revise or repeal where necessary) which result in the detention of persons because of their homosexual identity or homosexual acts in private between consenting adults. This review should also include any laws which result in imprisonment of advocates of homosexual rights.

- Stop the rape, sexual abuse and other torture and ill-treatment by governments of all persons, including lesbians and gay men. Cruel, inhuman or degrading treatment of persons in detention must be prohibited, including forcible "medical" treatment of lesbians or gay men in detention to change their sexual orientation.

- Stop the 'disappearance' and extra-judicial execution of lesbians and gay men by government agents. Governments must immediately work to halt these abuses by conducting prompt, thorough and impartial investigations of all reports of killings or 'disappearances' targeted at lesbians and gay men and bring those found responsible to justice.

- Abolish death penalty laws for all crimes, including those punishing homosexual acts or identity.

- Review laws and practices to ensure that torture, political killing, death threats and other grave harassment of persons, based on their sexual identity are promptly and impartially investigated, prosecuted and punished in the regular administration of justice. Particular attention should be paid to ensuring that human rights defenders, working to protect the rights of homosexuals, or whose work in the context of women's human rights or HIV/AIDS education brings them under attack as lesbians or gay men, are adequately protected.

- Ensure that information on the prohibition against torture, including rape and sexual abuse, are fully included in the training of all agents of government, including all law enforcement personnel, civil or military; medical personnel; public officials and others involved in custody, interrogation, arrest and detention or imprisonment of individuals, including in the context of refugee and asylum seekers. Special attention should be given to including protection of the rights of gay men and lesbians to be free of torture in all education efforts.

- Review and revise (or repeal where necessary) all barriers, whether in law or administrative practice, to persons seeking political asylum on the basis of persecution based on sexual identity. Such barriers to the internationally guaranteed right to seek asylum would include discriminatory or exclusionary laws targeted towards homosexual identity or unjustifiably linked to real or perceived HIV/AIDS status.

- Promote human rights education which emphasizes the need to protect the human rights of all persons, including lesbians and gay men.

- Work to ensure that protections for human rights are effectively advanced at all relevant UN conferences. For example, at the 4th World Conference on Women in Beijing in September 1995, governments should encourage the national, regional and international participation of grassroots groups working to protect lesbians' human rights and should include information on the protection of those rights in their national reports.

- Demonstrate their commitment to protecting the human rights of all persons, including lesbians and gay men, by ratifying the international instruments for the protection of human rights with as few limiting reservations as possible. These international instruments include the Covenant on Civil and Political Rights, the Covenant on Economic, Social and Cultural Rights, the Convention Against Torture and Other Cruel, Inhuman and Degrading Treatment or Punishment, the Convention on the Elimination of All Forms of Discrimination Against Women, the Convention on the Elimination of All Forms of Racial Discrimination and the Convention on the Rights of the Child. In submitting reports to the appropriate international and regional treaty-monitoring bodies, governments should include information on: the ability of lesbians and gay men to enjoy the relevant rights and freedoms; steps being taken at national and local levels to remove obstacles to the full enjoyment of rights and freedoms by lesbians and gay men; and provisions for their protection.

Footnotes

[1]We acknowledge that the words *gay, lesbian and bisexual* are predominantly Western terms which may not adequately or accurately define individuals who are oriented affectionally towards others of their own sex, particularly in non-Western cultures. The native American *berdache* and the Ghanaian *obaa banyin* are examples of other culturally relevant terms.

[2] Amnesty International, "Women on the Front Line: Human Rights Violations against Women" AI Index: ACT 77/01/91.

[3] Amnesty International, "Facing Up to the Failures: Proposals for Improving the Protection of Human Rights by the United Nations " AI Index: IOR 41/16/92

[4] Excerpt from presentation by Juan Pablo Ordonez at American Bar Association Annual Convention, New York, August 8, 1993.

[5] United Nations Document E/CN.4/1992/SR 21 at para. 35, as cited in "Token Gestures: Women's Human Rights and UN Reporting. The UN Special Rapporteur on Torture" (June 1993) The International Human Rights Law Group / Women in the Law Project.

Appendix:

UNIVERSAL DECLARATION OF HUMAN RIGHTS

Adopted and proclaimed by General Assembly resolution 217 A(III) of 10 December 1948

Preamble

Whereas recognition of the inherent dignity and of the equal and inalienable rights of all members of the human family is the foundation of freedom, justice and peace in the world,

Whereas disregard and contempt for human rights have resulted in barbarous acts which have outraged the conscience of mankind, and the advent of a world in which human beings shall enjoy freedom of speech and belief and freedom from fear and want has been proclaimed as the highest aspiration of the common people,

Whereas it is essential, if man is not to be compelled to have recourse, as a last resort, to rebellion against tyranny and oppression, that human rights should be protected by the rule of law,

Whereas it is essential to promote the development of friendly relations between nations,

Whereas the peoples of the United Nations have in the Charter reaffirmed their faith in fundamental human rights, in the dignity and worth of the human person and in the equal rights of men and women and have determined to promote social progress and better standards of life in larger freedom,

Whereas Member States have pledged themselves to achieve, in co-operation with the United Nations, the promotion of universal respect for and observance of human rights and fundamental freedoms,

Whereas a common understanding of these rights and freedoms is of the greatest importance for the full realization of this pledge,

Now, therefore,

The General Assembly

Proclaims this Universal Declaration of Human Rights as a common standard of achievement for all peoples and all nations. to the end that every individual and every organ of society, keeping this Declaration constantly in mind, shall strive by teaching and education to promote respect for these rights and freedoms and by progressive measures, national and international, to secure their universal and effective recognition and observance, both among the peoples of Member States themselves and among the peoples of territories under their jurisdiction.

Article 1

All human beings are born free and equal in dignity and rights. They are endowed with reason and conscience and should act towards one another in a spirit of brotherhood.

Article 2

Everyone is entitled to all the rights and freedoms set forth in this Declaration, without distinction of any kind, such as race, colour, sex, language, religion, political or other opinion, national or social origin, property, birth or other status.

Furthermore, no distinction shall be made on the basis of the political, jurisdictional or international status of the country or territory to which a person belongs, whether it be independent, trust, non-self-governing or under any other limitation of sovereignty.

Article 3

Everyone has the right to life, liberty and the security of person.

Article 4

No one shall be held in slavery or servitude, slavery and the slave trade shall be prohibited in all their forms.

Article 5

No one shall be subjected to torture or to cruel, inhuman or degrading treatment or punishment.

Article 6

Everyone has the right to recognition everywhere as a person before the law.

Article 7

All are equal before the law and are entitled without any discrimination to equal protection of the law. All are entitled to equal protection against any discrimination in violation of this Declaration and against any incitement to such discrimination.

Article 8

Everyone has the right to an effective remedy by the competent national tribunals for acts violating the fundamental rights granted him by the constitution or by law.

Article 9

No one shall be subjected to arbitrary arrest, detention or exile.

Article 10

Everyone is entitled in full equality to a fair and public hearing by an independent and impartial tribunal, in the determination of his rights and obligations and of any criminal charge against him.

Article 11

1. Everyone charged with a penal offence has the right to be presumed innocent until proved guilty according to law in a public trial at which he has had all the guarantees necessary for his defence.

2. No one shall be held guilty of any penal offence on account of any act or omission which did not constitute a penal offence, under national or international law, at the time when it was committed. Nor shall a heavier penalty be imposed than the one that was applicable at the time the penal offence was committed.

Article 12

No one shall be subjected to arbitrary interference with his privacy, family, home or correspondence, nor to attacks upon his honour and reputation. Everyone has the right to the protection of the law against such interference or attacks.

Article 13

1. Everyone has the right to freedom of movement and residence within the borders of each State.

2. Everyone has the right to leave any country, including his own, and to return to his country.

Article 14

1. Everyone has the right to seek and to enjoy in other countries asylum from persecution.

2. This right may not be invoked in the case of prosecutions genuinely arising from non-political crimes or from acts contrary to the purposes and principles of the United Nations.

Article 15

1. Everyone has the right to a nationality.

2. No one shall be arbitrarily deprived of his nationality nor denied the right to change his nationality.

Article 16

1. Men and women of full age, without any limitation due to race, nationality or religion, have the right to marry and to found a family. They are entitled to equal rights as to marriage, during marriage and at its dissolution.

2. Marriage shall be entered into only with the free and full consent of the intending spouses.

3. The family is the natural and fundamental group unit of society and is entitled to protection by society and the State.

Article 17

1. Everyone has the right to own property alone as well as in association with others.

2. No one shall be arbitrarily deprived of his property.

Article 18

Everyone has the right to freedom of thought, conscience and religion; this right includes freedom to change his religion or belief, and freedom, either alone or in community with others and in public or private, to manifest his religion or belief in teaching, practice, worship and observance.

Article 19

Everyone has the right to freedom of opinion and expression; this right includes freedom to hold opinions without interference and to seek, receive and impart information and ideas through any media and regardless of frontiers.

Article 20

1. Everyone has the right to freedom of peaceful assembly and association.

2. No one may be compelled to belong to an association.

Article 21

1. Everyone has the right to take part in the government of his country, directly or through freely chosen representatives.

2. Everyone has the right of equal access to public service in his country.

3. The will of the people shall be the basis of the authority of government; this will shall be expressed in periodic and genuine elections which shall be by universal and equal suffrage and shall be held by secret vote or by equivalent free voting procedures.

Article 22

Everyone, as a member of society, has the right to social security and is entitled to realization, through national effort and international co-operation and in accordance with the organization and resources of each State. of the economic. social and cultural rights indispensable for his dignity and the free development of his personality.

Article 23

1. Everyone has the right to work, to free choice of employment, to just and favourable conditions of work and to protection against unemployment.

2. Everyone, without any discrimination, has the right to equal pay for equal work.

3. Everyone who works has the right to just and favourable remuneration ensuring for himself and his family an existence worthy of human dignity, and supplemented, if necessary, by other means of social protection.

4. Everyone has the right to form and to join trade unions for the protection of his interests.

Article 24

Everyone has the right to rest and leisure, including reasonable limitation of working hours and periodic holidays with pay.

Article 25

1. Everyone has the right to a standard of living; adequate for the health and well-being of himself and of his family, including food, clothing, housing and medical care and necessary social services, and the right to security in the event of unemployment, sickness, disability, widowhood, old age or other lack of livelihood in circumstances beyond his control.

2. Motherhood and childhood are entitled to special care and assistance. All children, whether born in or out of wedlock, shall enjoy the same social protection.

Article 26

1. Everyone has the right to education. Education shall be free, at least in the elementary and fundamental stages. Elementary education shall be compulsory. Technical and professional education shall be made generally available and higher education shall be equally accessible to all on the basis of merit.

2. Education shall be directed to the full development of the human personality and to the strengthening of respect for human rights and fundamental freedoms. It shall promote understanding, tolerance and friendship among all nations, racial or religious groups, and shall further the activities of the United Nations for the maintenance of peace.

3. Parents have a prior right to choose the kind of education that shall be given to their children.

Article 27

1. Everyone has the right freely to participate in the cultural life of the community, to enjoy the arts and to share in scientific advancement and its benefits.

2. Everyone has the right to the protection of the moral and material interests resulting from any scientific, literary or artistic production of which he is the author.

Article 28

Everyone is entitled to a social and international order in which the rights and freedoms set forth in this Declaration can be fully realized.

Article 29

1. Everyone has duties to the community in which alone the free and full development of his personality is possible.

2. In the exercise of his rights and freedoms, everyone shall be subject only to such limitations as are determined by law solely for the purpose of securing due recognition and respect for the rights and freedoms of others and of meeting the just requirements of morality, public order and the general welfare in a democratic society.

3. These rights and freedoms may in no case be exercised contrary to the purposes and principles of the United Nations.

Article 30

Nothing in this Declaration may be interpreted as implying for any State, group or person any right to engage in any activity or to perform any act aimed at the destruction of any of the rights and freedoms set forth herein.

Amnesty International Needs Your Help

Human rights violations against gays and lesbians are often difficult to document. Fear of social ostracism and further abuse silences many homosexuals and their allies from speaking out against killings, torture, or imprisonment. Amnesty International considers for adoption anyone who is imprisoned:

- solely because of their homosexuality, including the practice of homosexual acts in private between consenting adults;
- for advocating homosexual equality;
- on charges of homosexuality when these have been used as a pretext and the real reason for their imprisonment is the expression of their political, religious or other conscientiously-held beliefs.

We also oppose the torture and execution of anyone, including those tortured and killed for their real or perceived homosexuality.

If you, or someone you know has fallen victim to such a violation, please send a detailed letter describing the abuse to:

Amnesty International
International Secretariat
1 Easton Street
London WCIX 8DJ
United Kingdom